Scottish Borders Library Service

KV-190-957

TION | 952.04

X

Mr. Tanaka
44 years old

Mrs. Tanaka
37 years old

Taro
14 years old

Akiko
8 years old

BIG BUSINESS... IN JAPAN

by
Anna Sproule

Hiroko
11 years
old

Granny Yamada
61 years old

Macdonald Educational

BORDERS REGIONAL LIBRARY

ACCESSION No. | CLASS No.
P 78572 | 952·04

What is this book about?

Sony, Toyota, Honda, Sanyo . . . These are just some of the names that mean big business in Japan. They are famous all over the world. All business is about exchanging things for money: the firm that makes things to sell, for example, and the shop that sells them are both in business. Japanese big business and the things it produces have helped to make Japan one of the world's richest countries.

How to use this book

Part of this book is a story. But, all through, you'll see sections like this one which look as if they've been torn from a reporter's notebook. They are marked 'Evidence'. All the pictures in these sections are of real people and of how they really lived and worked. They will show you how Japanese big business got started and how it has grown.

Factual Adviser
Toshi Marks
Centre for the Study of Contemporary Japan
Essex University

Educational Adviser
Alistair Ross
Principal Lecturer in Primary Education
Polytechnic of North London

Series and Book Editor Nicole Lagneau

Teacher Panel
Tim Firth, Lynn McCoombe, Lesley Snell

Design Sally Boothroyd

Production Rosemary Bishop

Picture Research Suzanne Williams

A MACDONALD BOOK

© Macdonald & Company (Publishers) Ltd 1986

First published in Great Britain in 1986 by Macdonald & Company (Publishers) Ltd, London & Sydney
A BPCC plc company
All rights reserved

Printed and bound in Great Britain by Purnell Book Production Ltd, Paulton, nr. Bristol

Macdonald & Co (Publishers) Ltd
Greater London House
Hampstead Road
London NW1 7QX

British Cataloguing in Publication Data
Sproule, Anna
Big business – in Japan.—(People then and now)
1. Japan—Social conditions—1945-
—Juvenile literature
I. Title   II. Series
952.04   HN723.5
ISBN 0-356-11230-6

Contents

Shopping	8– 9
House or flat?	10–11
Work and play	12–13
Comment: Big business	14–15
The red kimono	16–17
Super Express	18–19
Comment: Japanese revolution	20–21
Grandfather's way	22–23
A woman's job?	24–25
Comment: The old ways	26–27
Exam term	28–29
Roman letters	30–31
Comment: Learning	32–33
The news	34–35
Western things	36–37
Over the North Pole	38–39
Comment: The world outside	40–41
Find out more	42–43
Time chart and Keywords	44
Index	45

BORDERS
REGIONAL
LIBRARY

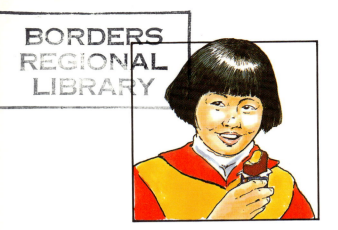

Shopping

Akiko stared at the cat. From the shop window the cat stared back with its china eyes, and beckoned to her with its china paw to come and buy something. Inside the shop were piles of snacks and sweets: some shaped like cars, and some like trees and some like umbrellas. Over the cat's head the shopkeeper had fixed a real umbrella – a tiny one of waxed paper – just for fun. What a clever idea, Akiko thought. Just the thing, on this dripping wet day. The umbrella sweets looked very nice too; yes, she'd have some. Quickly, she counted out some coins and handed them over. The shopkeeper bowed and gave her four sweets. Akiko bowed back and hurried out.

It was the last Saturday of the holidays, and they were all going into Tokyo together – Father, Mother, Taro, Hiroko and Akiko herself. It was really Taro's trip. He'd been saving for ages to buy a new camera, and they were now going to a special place in Tokyo to buy it. But then Mother had said she wanted to buy dinner first, in the shops by the station. It was going to be eel. 'What a thing to be taking to a place like Shinjuku,' Father joked. 'Never mind,' said Mother. 'It's cheaper out here in the suburbs.'

Father was right about Shinjuku. It was an odd place to be going to with a cooked eel for dinner. The shops were very smart, and so were the people. In the discount shops there were more cameras than Akiko had ever seen in her life. There were also home computers, calculators and watches. All sorts of people came and went.

Small business in Japan: a traditional greengrocer's shop around 1890. A great many Japanese people still work in small businesses like this shop and little factories. ▼

EVIDENCE

Big business in Japan: the Japanese people themselves are keen to buy electronic and other goods which are made in their factories.

All business, big or small, is about selling things. This china cat, with its beckoning paw, is an old Japanese custom of inviting shoppers to come and look at what there is for sale.

There were some westerners too, all buying and buying. Akiko found she was looking at rows and rows of watches, all very cheap: only 2000 yen. Well, she probably had that much; she'd brought her own savings with her, just in case. She got her purse out and starting counting: One thousand and eight hundred yen. That wasn't enough; she had forgotten the sweets. It was no use asking Mother. She was always so careful with money.

Going home from the station, Akiko saw the cat again in its shop window. 'It was your fault I bought the sweets,' she told it. But it just went on beckoning with its fat round china paw.

9

House or flat?

It went on raining and raining. 'But let's be thankful,' said Granny Yamada. 'At least, this autumn, there hasn't been a typhoon, so far.' Granny Yamada was Mother's mother. She lived quite close, one stop down the railway line, with her husband and her youngest daughter, Kyoko. She and Aunt Kyoko came to visit them a lot. In fact, Kyoko was here now talking to Mother about house-hunting; she'd got engaged last spring — but, she and her fiancé wanted to wait until they'd found somewhere to live before they got married.

'You'd think he'd help me look for a house,' Kyoko was saying. 'He knows I'd like a house rather than a company flat. But no — he just goes on saying we can rent a flat from his company to start with. I know it would be cheap — well, that's the point, isn't it? It's an extra something for company workers. But I don't want to see the other company wives every day — I hear plenty about the company as it is.'

House-hunting sounded difficult, Akiko thought as she finished another storey of her paper pagoda. She and Hiroko were having a race to see who could build a ten-storey pagoda quickest. Still listening, she reached for a new sheet of paper.

'What about that other flat you were looking at?' Mother was asking Aunt Kyoko. 'I know you don't like high-rise blocks, but surely it's better than nothing.' 'It was too high up,' said Aunt Kyoko gloomily. 'It just didn't feel right. I like living low down, in a proper old-fashioned house.' 'But in typhoons it's small buildings that get damaged,'

said Mother. 'Just think of the cost, too. If you started off in a company flat you could begin saving for a proper house. And you'd have money left for your skiing as well.' 'That's another thing,' Aunt Kyoko replied. 'He says he's not so keen on it now; he'd rather play golf. It will help him get on in business, he says. If he has to meet important people, he can take them golfing.'

Getting married sounded difficult, too, Akiko said to herself. But she knew how her aunt felt: a proper house was much nicer than a flat. She glanced across at her sister — and stared. Her pagoda looked all funny: it didn't stick out at the corners at all. Hiroko saw her looking, and smiled. 'High-rise block,' she said calmly. 'I just invented it; so I win'.

'No, you don't!' Akiko snapped. 'I'm worse than any typhoon!' She puffed out her cheeks and blew, and Hiroko's invention flew away across the room.

Homes for staff members of Japan Air Lines. Big companies often provide flats at low rents for their workers, because housing in Japan is expensive.

EVIDENCE

Japanese houses, even small ones like these traditional wooden homes, cost a lot of money. People who work in big companies can borrow money from their firms.

As big business has grown, many people in Japan have become richer. They now have money to spend on sports like skiing. ▶

Work and play

'Mother! *Okasan* – Mother! I won – did you see me? I won the race!' There was a pain in Akiko's side and her legs wobbled. But none of that mattered. She had always wanted to win the 100-metre running race in her school's autumn sports, and now she'd done it. Hiroko had seen it too, which was good; pity Father hadn't been there as well. Never mind – he'd be there tonight.

Father was an electronics engineer. He helped run a factory that made electronic parts. 'They're not for any one special thing,' he'd told Akiko once when she'd asked if he'd made the inside of Taro's radio. 'They can go into radios, or TVs, or computers, or even hearing aids – it depends on the size. It's the small ones that are the most interesting,' he'd added with a grin.

He went to work at seven in the morning and he got home at eight at night, or later. In between, he read reports on what the factory was doing, checked it was all going well, and sorted things out if there were problems. A lot of his work was done at meetings – with his boss, or people from other parts of the company, or with customers. 'And that's where he is now,' said Mother later, when she rang him to tell him about Akiko's race. 'He's at a meeting. He's going to be late back home, too.'

Akiko was just climbing into her bunk bed when Mother called her downstairs again. 'Telephone – for you,' she said, smiling. Akiko took it from her. 'Hallo,' she said into it; '*moshi, moshi*.' 'Who's our champion runner then?' said Father proudly.

These Honda workers have arrived early to talk about what they are going to do at work today. There are contests and prizes for specially good ideas.

Going home: railway guards wedge workers into a commuter train during the rush hour. Some journeys can take up to two hours each way. As Japanese workers get more and more prosperous, rush hours like this one seem a small price to pay.

Most workers in big Japanese companies spend all their working lives with one firm. They get paid different amounts at different ages. Can you see when they'd expect to earn most?

'Mother has told me. I've got to stay here all evening, so I thought I'd say it by 'phone. Well done – *omedeto*!' Akiko beamed, even though he couldn't see her. 'But where are you?' she asked. 'At a restaurant, with my boss. We've got a foreign customer here: he wanted to meet the man who liked making things small,' Father said. Akiko laughed happily. 'Omedeto to you,' she replied. 'Congratulations!' And Father thanked her warmly.

Next day, Father left for work at six, before Akiko was up. But he left something for her. It was a watch. 'We saw you looking at them in Shinjuku,' said Mother. 'Look – it'll measure lap times.' Akiko looked at the back of the watch closely. 'Made in Japan,' it said. Well – where else?

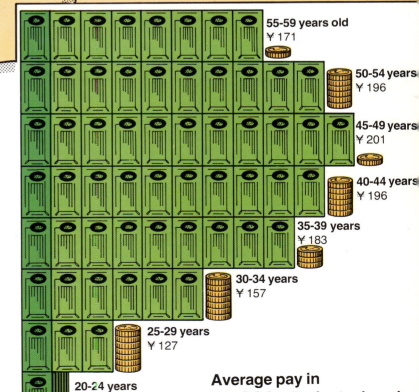

55-59 years old
¥ 171

50-54 years
¥ 196

45-49 years
¥ 201

40-44 years
¥ 196

35-39 years
¥ 183

30-34 years
¥ 157

25-29 years
¥ 127

20-24 years
¥ 100

Average pay in Yen (¥) for 5 minutes' work

Big business

Next time you're out shopping, take a special look at things like TV sets, video recorders, cameras, watches and calculators – and even the cars parked in the streets. The chances are that many of them were made by one of the big businesses of Japan. Some of these businesses are really huge: Hitachi, for example, employs over 150,000 people. Hundreds of thousands more work in the smaller businesses that make goods for the big firms. Together these companies have made Japan the second most important country in the world for producing manufactured goods.

Just after World War Two, none of this would have seemed possible. But, between 1955 and 1961, the country suddenly became twice as rich. Through the 1960s it went on getting richer much faster than other countries. One reason was that the Japanese have always bought the best factory equipment, so that things can be made more cheaply.

Also, Japanese families like saving money. Bank savings are lent again to businesses to use for buying better equipment. However, this is not the whole story behind Japan's 'economic miracle'. The country's past history has been important, too, and so has the way it has educated its people.

Part of Japan after World War Two. Millions were homeless and industry was in ruins.

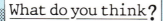

In 1966, world records were broken when the first ship ever to weigh more than 200,000 tons was launched in a Japanese shipyard. It was a supertanker called the *Idemitsu Maru* and measured 342 m. It was built in just nine months and named after its owner, oil millionaire Sazo Idemitsu. Like other Japanese businessmen, Mr Idemitsu believed in behaving like a father to his workers, paying for their homes, medical care and education. This system is called 'paternalism', and is different from the way many British firms treat their workers. Do you think paternalism would be a good idea in your country?

Thinking big in 1985: Sony's enormous TV screen, called the Jumbotron, draws the crowds at an exhibition of technology. ▼

The red kimono

Quite suddenly, Hiroko decided she didn't want to wear her kimono any more. She couldn't move in it, she said. Mother sighed and shook her head, and Granny Yamada tried scolding. But Hiroko just said she didn't care. So there was one nearly new silk kimono, waiting to be worn by someone else.

It was a beautiful kimono, too — bright red, with a pattern of flowers and flying birds. 'Flying cranes,' said Akiko, admiring them. 'Cranes to wish you a long life.' 'That's right,' said Granny Yamada, who was visiting. 'How nice that red would look on you. Let's see, now.' And she draped the kimono round Akiko's shoulders. 'Well,' she said to Mother, 'what do you think? With New Year coming and everything? She could do with a new kimono for that, you know.'

When Granny Yamada decided something, she liked to get things going quickly. That very day, she and Mother took Hiroko's kimono to pieces. Then they both started making the pieces into a kimono for Akiko. They turned bits in, and pinned bits up. They tried it on her, took it off, put it back on again. 'Keep still,' Granny Yamada told her sharply. 'If you don't, you'll spoil it. What lovely silk this is,' she continued, talking to Mother. 'Where did you say you got it?'

'It came from Tango,' Mother replied. 'Aah,' said Granny with a happy sigh. 'Tango silk; yes, it's always been famous. I remember my mother telling me about it, and she really knew about silk, coming from the family she did. Why, her mother —

16

Before western-style machinery came to Japan in the last century, silk was reeled from silkworm cocoons by hand. Selling silk abroad helped Japan to change into a modern country.

EVIDENCE

After Japan became modernised, silk could be reeled on factory machines like these. Modernisation started in the 1870s, after the emperor called Meiji came to power.

A century after western technology started coming to Japan, the country now leads the world in producing the most sophisticated machines of all: robots.

let's see, she was born the year of the Meiji Restoration, right back in 1868 . . .' 'That was your granny?' Akiko broke in, wide-eyed. Granny laughed, and patted her cheek. 'Yes, dear — I was someone's grand-daughter too, you know. Well, as I was saying; my granny was one of the best girls at reeling silk in the whole district. It was all done by hand then, of course — it was very delicate work, very delicate indeed. Only women could do it. But they made Japan famous all over the world: without them, there would have been no Japanese silk, and no western money to help the Emperor make all his big changes. Just think of that — my own little granny helping the Emperor.

Although —' and Granny Yamada chuckled — 'it was a good thing, wasn't it, that the silkworms in Europe had all fallen ill just then?' Akiko was puzzled for a second; then she suddenly understood, and chuckled too.

At last, the kimono was ready. Mother put a flower in Akiko's hair. Granny Yamada wound the long sash twice round Akiko's waist, tied it, tied a silk cord over that, and sat back on her heels. 'There,' she said. 'That looks beautiful; fit for an emperor's court. Go and look.' Akiko tottered over to the mirror, looked, and gasped. She bowed to herself and, smiling, her reflection bowed back.

17

Super Express

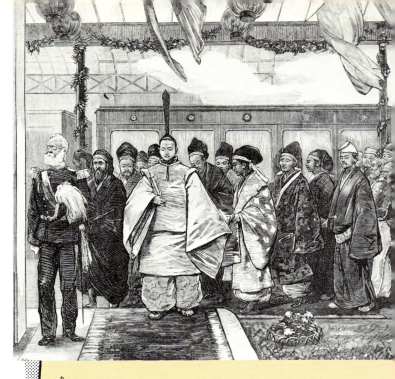

'Taro! Hiroko! Come along, now — follow the flag.' Mother set off through the crowds at Tokyo Central Station. Everyone seemed to be on the move that day. New Year was only three days off, and the station was full of people going to Nagoya, Kyoto, Osaka, Kobe, and all the places further on, to spend the holiday with their families.

The Shinkansen Super Express would be taking them all there, travelling at 210 km/h. Just over three hours to Osaka, thought Hiroko, trying to do sums in her head. So Osaka, where Father's parents lived, was . . . 'Come on — follow the flag.' said Mother again.

Four years after he came to power, the young Emperor Meiji opened Japan's first railway line in 1872. This picture was drawn by a western artist of the time.

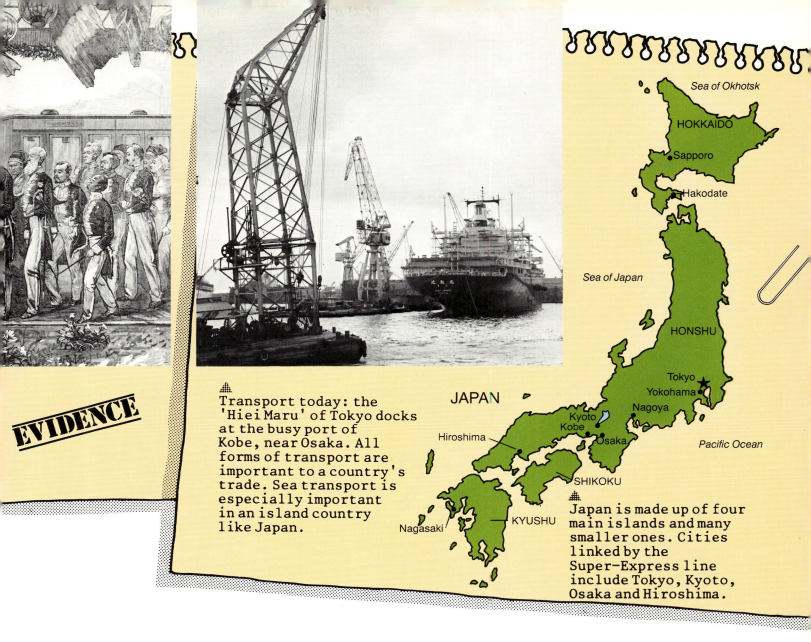

EVIDENCE

Transport today: the 'Hiei Maru' of Tokyo docks at the busy port of Kobe, near Osaka. All forms of transport are important to a country's trade. Sea transport is especially important in an island country like Japan.

JAPAN

Sea of Okhotsk

HOKKAIDO

Sapporo

Hakodate

Sea of Japan

HONSHU

Tokyo
Yokohama

Nagoya

Kyoto
Kobe
Osaka

Pacific Ocean

Hiroshima

SHIKOKU

Nagasaki

KYUSHU

Japan is made up of four main islands and many smaller ones. Cities linked by the Super-Express line include Tokyo, Kyoto, Osaka and Hiroshima.

Following the flag was a family joke, started by Father. It meant 'Come on, stick together,' and went back to the days before Mother and he were married. She had been a tour-guide then, taking groups of holiday-makers around. Father first met her when she had led a trip organised by his firm.

Leaders always carry a flag, so that you can see where they are. But Mother didn't work any more – 'I couldn't do that and look after you all too,' she'd said when Hiroko had once asked why. 'And I've forgotten everything I knew, I expect.'

Very smoothly, the train set off. Almost at once, they were rushing through the station for Yokohama – 'Japan's biggest port for trade with other countries,' said Mother. They didn't stop until Nagoya, and then there was only one more stop before Shin-Osaka itself: Kyoto, the old capital city.

'It's beautiful,' said Mother dreamily as it came into sight. 'It was my favourite place for tours. You remember, Hiroko – you've been there yourself with your school.' Hiroko nodded. Then she had a sudden thought. 'How far is it from Tokyo to Osaka?' she asked abruptly. Mother blinked. 'How far is it?' Hiroko asked again. 'Let's see, now,' said Mother, frowning. 'It's . . . yes, that's it! It's 515 kilometres.' 'There,' Hiroko told her. 'You haven't forgotten everything, after all.'

Japanese Revolution

In most western countries people changed over fairly slowly from earning their living by doing jobs at home to earning it in factories, shops and offices. The change started around 1780 and, over the next century, people also started to use a lot of the things we have in modern life, such as railways, free education for all, and a postal system. This also happened gradually. But Japan got many of these things all at once, along with western-style mines, spinning mills, shipyards and other industries. This 'Japanese Revolution' took place in little over 10 years.

It started in 1868. Before then, Japan had been closed to foreigners for many years. But a revolt took power away from the *shoguns*, the generals who ran the country, and gave it to Emperor Meiji.

The Emperor wanted to make Japan as powerful as the countries of the west, with money to pay for a strong modern army. Trade from the new industries grew fast and, by 1900, Japan's wealth had trebled. By 1920 it had almost doubled again, and again by 1930. Although the industries were ruined in World War Two, the people who rebuilt them so quickly afterwards were helped by knowing what had been done earlier.

Emperor Meiji and his wife in western clothes for an official photograph. His real name was Mutsuhito. His coming to the throne is called the 'Meiji Restoration' because power was taken away from the shoguns (military rulers) and restored to the emperor.

Tokyo around 1800. Then, only a few foreign traders were allowed into Nagasaki.

What do you think?

When technology develops very quickly, the old equipment and way of thinking are often forgotten. But this hasn't happened to the traditional Japanese abacus or *soroban*, used here by businessmen discussing a deal. People use a soroban everywhere in Japan — even to check sums done on a calculator! The use of the abacus is at least 1400 years old. Try asking someone who's quick with an abacus, if you know one, why they think the Japanese still use it.

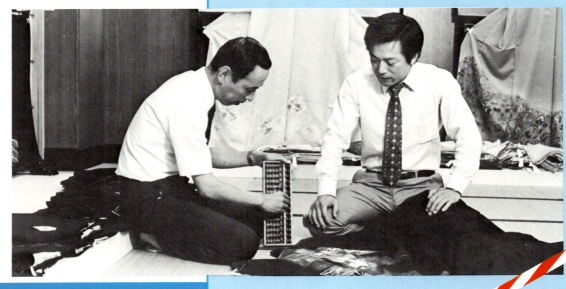

Grandfather's way

Granny and Grandfather Tanaka were old-fashioned, and they lived in an old-fashioned way. Old Mr Tanaka was proud of it. 'In this house, we follow traditions,' he'd say. 'We do things in the real Japanese way. We have order and calm and proper respect, too: respect for your grandfather, please.' But he always smiled when he said it. Hiroko thought he was going to say something else on New Year's morning, when they all went to the shrine and she wore a dress rather than a kimono. But he didn't say anything, so that was all right. Sleeping in the traditional way was all right, too; it was quite fun to sleep on the floor on big mattresses. But there was something Taro and Hiroko didn't enjoy at all, and that was the old-fashioned New Year's meal they were going to have.

It was real traditional New Year food, and Granny Tanaka had spent hours and hours making it. Taro and Hiroko knew just what it was going to be like. 'It's the black beans I can't stand,' Hiroko said. 'Well, I'd rather eat them than Granny's *mochi*,' Taro replied. Mochi were rice cakes. They were round and smooth and white, and very, very sticky. You had them toasted, in soup.

'Why can't they let us have hamburgers instead?' Taro went on. Hiroko giggled and screwed up her eyebrows like old Mr Tanaka. 'In this house . . .,' she began. But Taro didn't find it at all funny. Hiroko didn't find it funny either, later on, when they all sat down to their special New Year lunch. It was a hard job eating it all. But, with Grandfather Tanaka there, Hiroko and Taro had to do their best.

'Wherever have you been?' Granny Tanaka asked them both the next day. 'Oh, just out,' Taro replied carefully. Mother looked at them, then suddenly wrinkled her nose and sniffed.

'All right,' she hissed when Granny had trotted out of the kitchen for a minute. 'I can smell them – chips. You naughty children, couldn't you wait till we got home? It's so rude, so disrespectful. You know we do things Grandfather's way here – what would he say if he knew? We had enough trouble as it is over your kimono, Hiroko – Granny had to beg him not to say anything . . .'

They hung their heads as Mother went on and on. But, through it all, Hiroko could still remember the glorious taste of the stuff she and Taro had bought from the food bar two blocks away. Pity they'd forgotten to wipe the grease off their fingers properly. All the same, a telling off was only a scolding. And chips were chips.

EVIDENCE

In traditional life in
Japan, all the family
took part in businesses
like silk rearing. Your
grandfather was also
your boss!

In modern families, the
father still gets the 'seat
of honour' at table, with his
back to the alcove where
seasonal scrolls and flowers
are placed.

23

A woman's job?

That evening, they played *karuta*, the hundred-poem card game. Grandfather Tanaka said he was too old for such excitements, and would be the caller instead. 'Oh yes,' Granny Tanaka replied. 'You do it so well, too.' Hiroko remembered they'd said exactly the same thing last year.

You needed 200 cards to play karuta. They were arranged in two sets of 100 cards each. One set had complete poems with pictures. This is the one Grandfather had. He was the caller. The second half of the poems was in the other set, the one for the players. Father was dealing that set out. While he did it, Mother went on chatting to Granny Tanaka. They were talking about Aunt Kyoko, who'd managed to find a first-floor flat at last. 'But February — that's a horrible month for a wedding,' said Granny. 'It's her fiancé,' said Mother. 'He's going on a course in the spring — salesman's English, you know; his company's running it. And he'd like to get the wedding out of the way before he starts.'

Granny pursed her lips. 'Ah — well, that's different, then. Of course she must fit in; if he's got to study then, he'll want peace and calm. And it'll be nice for her to be there and help him — that's our job, after all, isn't it?' And she smiled at Hiroko, who was listening, open-mouthed. 'But —' Hiroko began. Mother stopped her. 'Now, Hiroko,' she said warningly. 'Granny is just saying how important it is for a woman to work hard at looking after her husband and family.' 'Oh yes — and the family too,' said Granny Tanaka, still smiling. 'Now that really is

our job — bringing up our children and seeing they're always well and happy.' 'But —' Hiroko objected again. 'Hush, Hiroko-*chan*,' said Mother hurriedly. 'Look — Grandfather is ready to start.'

'In the rain the flower's colour is fading,' Grandfather read from the first card in his set. 'Got it!' Taro cried; he had the second bit of the poem among his own cards. The matching pair was put on one side, and Grandfather read another poem. The game went very fast; you really had to be quick to win at karuta, thought Hiroko as for the third time she missed a card she ought to have seen. Both Taro and Father were very quick indeed. But Granny Tanaka was even quicker.

Suddenly, Hiroko knew that Granny had almost won. At just the same moment, she saw Granny look round the game and realise the same thing. And then, as Hiroko watched in horror, Granny started missing card after card. Four more poems, and Father had caught up with her; six more, and the game was over. 'Omedeto!' Granny told him, with a bow. And she was smiling more happily than ever.

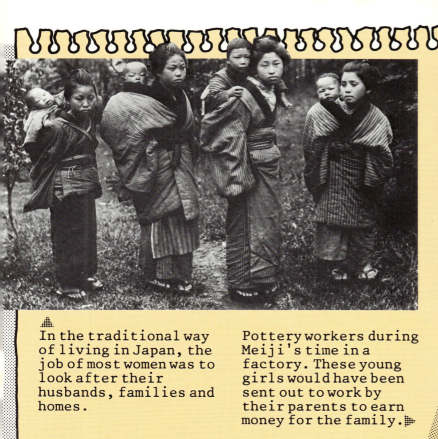

In the traditional way of living in Japan, the job of most women was to look after their husbands, families and homes.

Pottery workers during Meiji's time in a factory. These young girls would have been sent out to work by their parents to earn money for the family.

EVIDENCE

Dress designer Hanae Mori, one of the few Japanese women who have reached the top in their career. Most Japanese people still think a woman's main work is to have children and run the home for her family.

The old ways

In Britain, most people work between 35 and 40 hours a week. In Japan, it's more like 43 hours. Most workers are ready to put in a lot of overtime, and they often don't take all the holidays they're allowed. One reason for these long hours is quite simple: if you want to do well and get a top job, you must show you're keen! But Japanese workers also feel a much closer link with their firms than British ones do. If they think the company needs them to do something, they're proud to meet the company's need. Attitudes like these — being ready to work hard, to think of yourself as part of a group, and to put the group's needs first — have played an important part in making Japanese business big.

It all started before Meiji's time, in the days when Japan was mainly a nation of small family farmers. There is little good farming land in Japan and, to grow enough food to live on, you had to work very hard and work together. The father of the family was boss, but he tried to make decisions that helped the whole family. Only one-tenth of Japanese people get their living from farming now, but the old ways of working hard and obeying the boss are still followed. Without them, the economic miracle might not have happened.

What do you think?

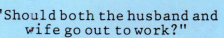
"Should both the husband and wife go out to work?"

Two recent surveys in Japan asked what people thought of wives going out to work. The results show that most Japanese men — even young ones — still think that a woman's main job in life is to run the home and leave men free to put all their energies into work. This attitude certainly allows Japanese male workers to spend long hours at work without worrying about domestic problems. But do you agree with it? And can you see what nearly half the young women in the survey thought? What do you think older women would have replied, if they'd been asked the same questions?

🟥 No response

🟧 Both husband and wife should go out to work, and both should cooperate with housework.

🟨 The husband should go out to work. The wife should also work as long as this does not interfere with housework.

🟩 The husband should work while the wife devotes herself entirely to housework.

New company employees (Male University graduates)

- 30.1%
- 57.1%
- 12.4%
- 0.4%

Women students at four-year universities.

- 9.0%
- 42.0%
- 43.2%
- 5.8%

◀ Japan's main crop, and its most important food, is rice. Rice must be planted in flooded 'paddies' like these. Everyone in the village needed to work together as a team, to make and flood them.

A master craftsman watches a worker decorate a vase around 1900. An apprentice working for him would show him very great respect. When Japan was modernised, workers still showed the same respect to their company bosses. ▶

Exam term

'T-A-N-A-K-A.' Hiroko drew the letters with care on a piece of paper. She drew 'HISOKO' next, and looked at it. Was that right? Well, Taro would know. They were difficult, these *Roma-ji* letters of the alphabet she'd learn at school in the spring. Taro said they were called after Rome, in Europe.

It was the last term of the school year. Outside, it was trying to snow. Going to Osaka and playing karuta all seemed ages ago. Now it was almost exam time for everybody: end-of-year exams, which were very important. Hiroko had exams in subjects like Japanese, and social studies, and arithmetic. It was to make a change from her homework that she asked Taro to show her how to write English words.

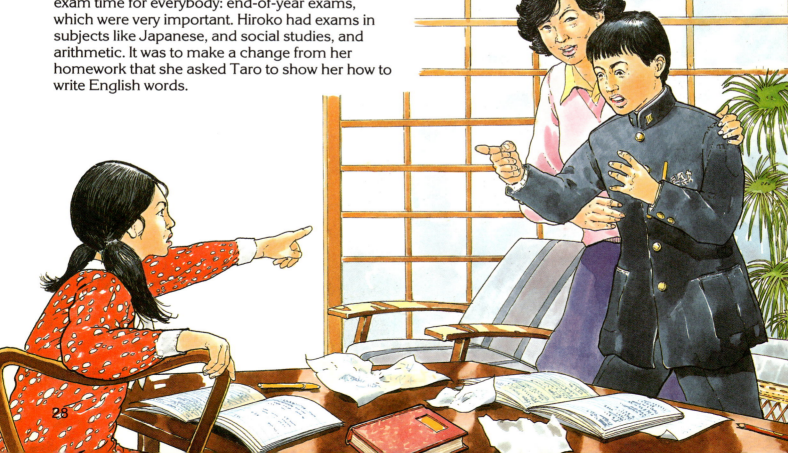

These children are doing the homework they've been set at a private school (or 'juku') on the train taking them home. It is after 9 pm. It is very important for Japanese children to do well in their school examinations so many parents pay for them to do extra schooling (and extra homework) each night.

Japanese girls do the same exams as boys, and do just as well. But there are many fewer girls than boys at universities. They are encouraged to think of marriage as their main career. Flower arranging is taught as an important home-making skill.

And it was to make a change for Taro — who had exams in English too — that he had stopped trying to revise and had taught her instead. But he was now in a bad mood. He just took one look at her piece of paper, and laughed. 'Hisoko, Hisoko,' he mocked, hissing the S's. 'Who's she? You've got it all wrong, anyway — it's "Hiroko Tanaka". I told you that; I told you they did it the other way round.' 'But you didn't —' Hiroko began. 'I did!' Taro shouted, and tore the paper across, and across again. Hiroko yelled back at him, and then Mother came rushing in.

'Poor Taro,' said Mother later, as she stirred the soup she was making. 'It's his exams, you know that.' 'But I've got them too,' Hiroko objected.

'And it's not till next year that he does the big ones.' 'A year isn't long,' said Mother firmly. 'He's got a lot to do. It's all so important for a boy — getting to high school and then university and then into a good job. And it all depends on his school exams. There isn't a second chance when he's grown-up. It's easier for you.' 'But there isn't a second chance for me either!' said Hiroko. 'I want a good job, too — you got one, after all. And I'll keep on with mine, not give it up. I'll be a —'

'You'll get married and have a family,' said Mother. 'Oh, Hiroko, why do you always want to be different? It'll make you unhappy some day. Why can't you be more like Akiko?' 'Oh, Mother!' Hiroko screeched, enraged. But Mother just went on stirring the soup.

Roman letters

Taro did well in his exams, after all. The month before, Aunt Kyoko got married, went on a skiing honeymoon, and cheered up. The cherry blossom came out in the parks and everyone went to photograph it. The new school year began, the one with the really big exams at the other end.

'Hiroko, I can't. Not with all this. Look at what I've got to do.' Taro pointed at the pile of history books. History was bad, Hiroko thought. There was so much to remember: dates and wars and who said what when. 'I can't,' Taro repeated. 'Mother's going to give me a test in a minute. Go on — go away.' He started muttering dates to himself — '1952, US occupation ends . . .' Hiroko left him to it.

She knew a lot of the Roma-ji letters by now. To make it easier, she had cut out the shapes in paper and hung them at the end of her bunk, like rows of washing. 'What a good idea,' Mother said. 'You'll see them every morning when you wake up.' But the paper shapes kept curling up and, in the end, Hiroko decided she'd have to make them solid, like the big letters she'd seen on the fronts of shops and offices in Tokyo. Taro belonged to a model-making club, so he ought to know how to do it. But now he was too busy to be bothered with her. Well, she'd have to work out how to do it.

This was something schools didn't teach you. They taught dates and facts and words, but they didn't show you how to solve puzzles and problems. And this was like a puzzle. Would it help if she made a lot of folded paper boxes and stuck them together?

Or how about cardboard boxes? What did they look like when you took them apart?

'Well, I never,' said Granny Yamada. 'And what does it say again?' '"Hiroko" — just "Hiroko"; I'll do the other Roma-ji shapes later.' Or maybe I won't, Hiroko said to herself. Making letters like tiny cardboard boxes was harder than she'd thought; she'd had to get Father to help her.

'What's that black square you've painted on?' Granny asked. 'It shows there's a hole in the O.' 'Well!' said Granny again .'They never taught you that in school, I'm sure. That's not education, that's play.' Oh well, Hiroko thought; but, at least, Father had understood. 'You worked that out yourself?' he'd asked. 'Omedeto! If you'd been at work, you'd have won a prize. Firms give them, you know, for original ideas. Trouble is, a lot of Japanese aren't taught to think in an original way.' So it didn't matter about being different then. In fact, when that good job came along, it might even be a help.

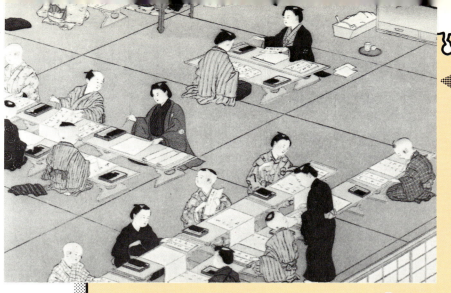

Even in traditional Japan, many people learned how to read and write. There were 50,000 schools like this already by the 1850s.

First day at school in the 1960s. Many pupils in Japanese first schools still sit in neat rows today. ▼

EVIDENCE

A bookshop in Tokyo. Publishing is another big business in Japan. Almost everyone likes to read a lot. ▼

Learning

Most Japanese children first go to school at the age of six. This is a year later than in Britain. They change school at 12, and they could leave altogether at 15. But most of them don't. In 1984, for instance, almost all 15-year-olds in Japan's middle schools decided to go on to high school, where they will stay until they are 18. From the start of schooling, pupils take exams every term.

The exam to get into high school is especially important, and so are the exams held at the end of high school to decide who goes to universities and colleges. In Japan, anyone who wants a good job in business or the government must have been to one of the best universities. So the working lives of all adults are dependent on exam success at school. This system makes it more likely that big business gets people who are used to hard work, willing to do what's expected of them, and good at remembering lots of facts.

Japanese education has aimed at producing people like this for a hundred years. It helped Japan to become a modern industrial country. But many Japanese people now feel that education should give them more encouragement to think things out for themselves and to do whatever they're best at.

UNIVERSITY
18-22 YEARS

JOBS IN BIG BUSINESS
22 YEARS – RETIREMENT

FIRST SCHOOL
6-12 YEARS

MIDDLE SCHOOL
12-15

EXAMINATION

HIGH SCHOOL
15-18

EXAMINATION

The Japanese Education System

What do you think?

People often say the Japanese education system is like an escalator. You get on at the bottom, aged six, and, if you work hard, it will take you all the way to university and a good job for life.

But there are two places where pupils can fall off the escalator or choose to get off and try another one. Can you see the places in the diagram? Most pupils pass into high school. Those who don't, go to technical training school or out to work. Students who do not get to university, or don't want to, can do a shorter course at a junior college. Many more girls do this than boys. Can you think why?

The 15-year-old with a cap on is leaving middle school. His friends 'bump' him to wish him luck. Most pupils now go on to training school or high school (see Japanese system above). Fewer than one child in twenty goes straight into jobs.

Things become easier once pupils get into university. They will automatically get a degree — and an executive's job for life.

The news

It was Akiko who went to the telephone. '*Moshi, moshi,*' she said into it, just as she always did. 'Who do you wish to speak to, please?' The person at the other end said he wanted Tanaka-*san*: Father. It was probably someone from his company. Akiko nearly said that he was on holiday. Then she realised it didn't sound polite. So she went to get him.

He, Taro and Hiroko were all watching a programme about elephants on afternoon TV. It was too hot to do anything but sit still and, now that school had stopped, Taro wasn't so busy. 'Just turn it up a bit,' Father was saying to Hiroko, who had the control set. 'That's — oh, it's for me, is it?' He got up and hurried out.

He was gone a long time. When he came back, Mother came with him. She glanced at the television; hastily, Hiroko switched it off. Then Father cleared his throat. 'We have some news for you,' he said slowly. 'That was my boss on the 'phone. He's got a new job for me, a very important job: he wants me to help start a new factory. It's in Britain — in England.' The children stared at him. 'But . . .' Taro began.

'I will be going to live in England for a while,' Father went on. 'But,' Taro started again, 'Why England? It's so small. America's much more important.' Father smiled. 'For Japan, yes,' he said. 'But England's where they want me to go, all the same.' 'But what about us? Can we come too?' This time, it was Mother who answered: 'Next year you will —

you and Hiroko; the company will pay for you to come and see us.'

'Us?' said Taro and Hiroko together. Mother looked upset. 'Yes; yes, I know. But I can't leave poor Father alone out there, can I? I'll be going too, with Akiko, next spring, after your exams — don't worry, Taro, I'm not going to abandon you before then. Nor you, Hiroko.' 'But afterwards?' asked Hiroko in a voice that wobbled. 'Well, Granny Yamada has room now that Kyoko's married; we thought . . .' Then Mother noticed Hiroko's expression. 'Or perhaps you could go to Granny Tanaka's,' she went on quickly. 'You like it in Osaka, don't you?'

Miserably, Hiroko nodded. She wasn't sure she liked it in Osaka all that much. But Granny Tanaka was nice — and anything was better than living at Granny Yamada's, even with Taro there too.

'Oh, Father!' Akiko wailed suddenly. 'You're not really going, are you? You don't really want to go?' Father looked at her. 'But, Akiko-*chan*,' he said, very seriously, 'I do. I love my family, and I love my job. If I get a better position, that makes things better for all of you, do you see? So I do want to go — I want to go very much. You'll be coming too, don't forget. You wait — you'll like it in England.'

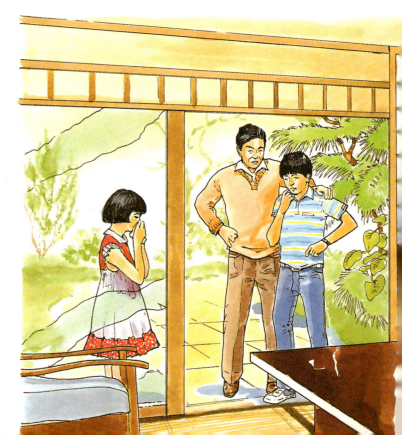

EVIDENCE

In 1853, America made Japan allow westerners into the country again to enable them to supply their ships and to trade. The demand was brought by Commodore Matthew Perry (left) — seen here as drawn by a Japanese.

The Occupation forces go shopping for souvenirs: US soldiers in Tokyo after World War Two. American money aid helped Japan to rebuild its wrecked homes and industries, and to start up in business again.

A modern American takes his Sony Walkman for a stroll. Today, America buys more Japanese goods than any other country.

Western things

Father left in October. He wrote to them all each week, and sent pictures of what England looked like. 'Look at the horses, Taro,' said Akiko, holding one up. But Taro just went on glaring at his book. His big exams, Akiko knew, would happen next term. He was working harder and harder and saying less and less. Hiroko worked hard too, but she had her own way of doing things and never even looked tired. Taro had black rings under his eyes.

'He should get more sleep,' said Granny Yamada one day. 'He can't,' said Mother fiercely.' 'He's got to study.' 'Well, he should have a change, go out more, then,' Granny went on. 'He can't,' said Mother again. 'And he won't, anyway.' 'No time for this, no time for that,' Granny Yamada grumbled. 'I tell you, he'll be ill if he goes on like this — or worse. You'll be saying he's got no time to eat next.' Mother stared at her. 'All right,' she said at last. 'We'll start on Sunday.' 'Start what?' Akiko asked. 'Never you mind,' said Mother.

Inside the food bar, Granny Yamada looked round in bewilderment. 'Taro-*chan* — you know these places; what do we do now?' Taro picked up a tray and gave it to her. 'You choose what you want,' he said. 'That's pizza, and those are chips, and that's ordinary soup with noodles.' 'I'll have soup,' said Granny. 'I won't have anything foreign.'

'But it's delicious — really it is,' said Mother, helping herself. 'Anyway, it's what they eat in England, so I've got to start getting used to it.'

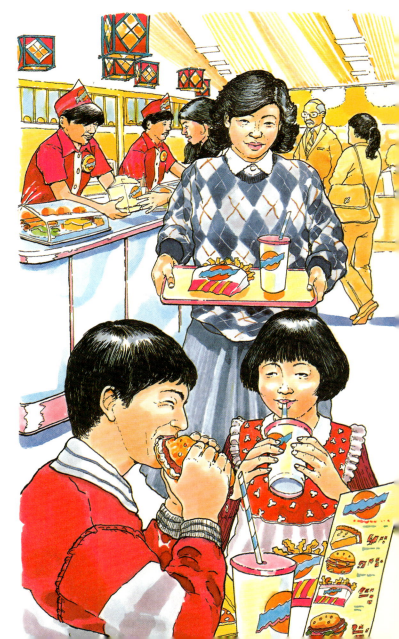

Both traditional and western means of transport are used in this Yokohama street after World War One. Japan now does bigger business in exporting motor vehicles than any other country.

Japan has a parliament or Diet elected by the people, like this voter. The first Diet was a western idea copied by people in the Meiji period.▶

Since Meiji's time, Japan has watched the west carefully to spot the latest trends. Today's 1950s revival and leather jackets are as popular with young people in Tokyo as they are in Britain. ▼

Every Sunday after that, Mother chose a new place for them to go to. They were all different, but they all sold western food: hamburgers, or pizza, or fried chicken, or ice-cream. Sometimes they ate in the shop and sometimes in the park. Granny Yamada often came with them. 'Oh dear – I don't like that,' she said when she first saw them eating hamburgers. 'Using your hands.' 'Oh, Granny!' said Taro impatiently. 'Well, dear, I'll try; they must do it over there, after all. We do so many western things, I just can't keep up.'

'Just a minute; I want another photo.' For the first time in ages, Taro had brought his camera out. 'If it comes out well, I'll send it to Father. Don't finish that yet, Granny!' 'Dear me,' said Granny Yamada with a giggle. 'Eating buns in the park, whatever next?' Behind Taro, Mother laughed too – and quietly dropped the rest of her hamburger in a litter bin. Akiko saw her. 'What . . .?' she began, when Mother quickly shook her head and whispered 'Ssh!' Well, how strange, Akiko thought. If Mother didn't like hamburgers, what on earth had they been doing all this time?

Over the North Pole

Mother bowed for the last time, then turned. 'Come along, Akiko-*chan*,' she said. 'Follow the flag.' Akiko set off beside her, walking along with all the other people catching the flight from Narita Airport to London, via Alaska. Just once, she looked back — and there they still were: Granny Yamada and her husband, Taro and Hiroko, Grandfather and Granny Tanaka, who would be taking Hiroko back to Osaka. She had done very well in her exams, and so had Taro. Looking very solemn, Hiroko gave her sister a tiny wave. Akiko waved back.

After Alaska, the plane took them north. 'This is the bit where we go over the North Pole,' said Mother.

'It's the shortest way.' Akiko nodded sleepily. She felt odd; almost as if there were two of her. One of them was sitting up here in the sunshine. The other was still at home in Tokyo, eating rice crackers and getting a last lesson in Roma-ji.

'Come on — that's an easy one,' Hiroko was saying, pointing at the can she'd taken from the fridge. 'You know it, anyway. What's the first letter? C-O-C-A . . . . . yes, that's it; come on . . . .'

'Akiko, wake up! We're there!' And so they were: at Heathrow in England on a cold March morning. They spent ages in one queue, then in another. Then, quite suddenly, they came out into a long corridor and there was Father waiting for them. At last, they had really arrived.

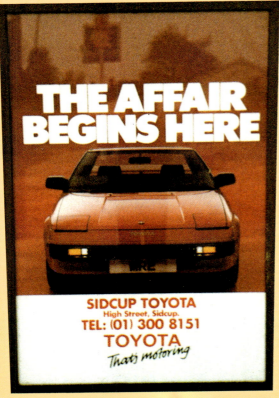

THE AFFAIR BEGINS HERE

SIDCUP TOYOTA
High Street, Sidcup.
TEL: (01) 300 8151
TOYOTA
That's motoring

Toyota cars, produced by the biggest of the giant Japanese car manufacturers, have arrived in Sidcup, Kent, in England.

But it still took a long time to get into London. From the bus window, Akiko stared crossly at the blue truck in front. It had been there for ages. For something to do, she spelt out the name on the back. 'T-O-Y . . .' It was Japanese. And there was another one. And what was that, on that big poster? 'Father – look!' she said, pointing. 'Clever girl,' said Father.

'What does that say, over there?' He pointed to a sign over a restaurant. Akiko took one look, and beamed; she knew it already. 'Breakfast!' she said. 'Oh, no!' Mother had seen it too. 'Don't worry,' Father told her. 'You can probably just have fried eggs.' 'Like at home,' Akiko said. 'England's just like home.' Father laughed. 'Well – not quite,' he said. 'You wait and see.'

Mrs Yoko Nakamura joining her son, Hiroki, for English language lessons in Washington, Tyne and Wear, after the local education authority started courses for wives and children of the executives of Nissan. The Japanese company is building a car plant in the town.

Japanese children from the age of four are being joined in the classrooms by their mothers. The headmistress of Eyton Primary School, Mrs Joan Wilson, has two mothers under her wing.

"They are doing very well. It is obvious that they want to integrate and are doing so with great success," she said.

Local food stores are considering opening a special department for their Japanese customers.

Source: The Times Newspaper, 26 June 1985, London

As this cutting from The Times newspaper shows, Japan also exports people – and jobs. Thousands of Britons work in Japanese firms in the UK.

39

The world outside

Japan, like Britain, is a small island country close to a huge continent, and its links with both that continent and others have been vital to the way its history has developed. It was hard to get to by sailing ship, but the Korean peninsula made a good 'stepping stone'. So it was through Korea that, almost 1600 years ago, Japan got its first writing system.

Other things like guns, playing cards, and some of Japan's favourite ways of cooking were brought by the Portuguese. They were the first Europeans to reach Japan in the 1500s. After the Meiji Restoration, Japan decided to learn all it could from the west. When its own new industries got under way, it quickly became an important world power. After World War Two, it rebuilt its industries and, today, only the USA is a bigger producer of manufactured goods.

Something else is happening as well. Japan's big businesses are getting more efficient all the time and other countries are finding it very hard to compete. What happens if Japan gets too efficient and too rich? Here is what its Prime Minister, Yasuhiro Nakasone, said in 1985: 'If you keep winning, nobody plays with you any more.' No-one is yet sure how to help the other manufacturing countries of the world to start winning again.

Coca Cola goes West: America's most famous drink is on sale at the 1964 Tokyo Olympics.

IMPORTS

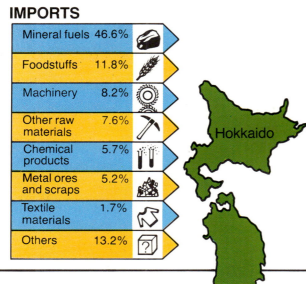

Mineral fuels	46.6%	
Foodstuffs	11.8%	
Machinery	8.2%	
Other raw materials	7.6%	
Chemical products	5.7%	
Metal ores and scraps	5.2%	
Textile materials	1.7%	
Others	13.2%	

EXPORTS

Machinery	67.8%	
Metal and metal products	12.5%	
Chemical products	4.7%	
Textile fibres	4.5%	
Non metal mineral products	1.5%	
Foodstuffs	0.9%	
Others	8.1%	

Like other countries, Japan is both a buyer and a seller. It buys goods it does not have, and sells goods it has in large amounts. Can you see which kinds of goods it sells the most?

JAPAN

Hokkaido

Honshu

Shikoku

Kyushu

Lined up and ready for export. Half of the motorcycles that Japan makes are sold abroad. The same is true of its colour televisions.

What do you think?

Taking the game seriously: the large heads on these young golfers' practice clubs are to improve their style. Golf is something else which has been brought in from western countries. It has become very popular in Japan. Over 15 million people now play it. But pursuing their sport is difficult: there are only 1400 courses in all the country, and club membership fees are very high.

How do you think these children feel about practising a sport they may never have much chance to play?

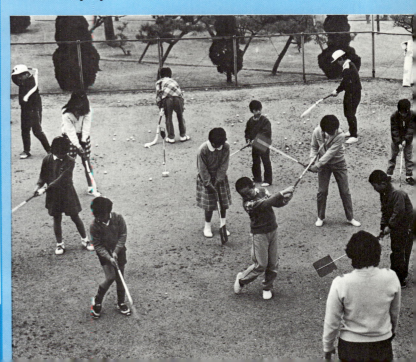

Find out more

In one way, this book has mainly been a story. But the things that happen to the family are real things that could happen to real Japanese people.

In the late 1800s, Japan quickly transformed itself from a country with old ideas and following traditional ways of living, to one with new ideas and a way of life based on industrial success. In this century, it recovered even more quickly from national disaster, and performed its 'economic miracle'. This book shows some of the reasons why the miracle happened. It also points to the problems that have come with making the miracle work. Akiko, Hiroko and Taro all face some of these problems. Can you say what they are? Do you think they solve them?

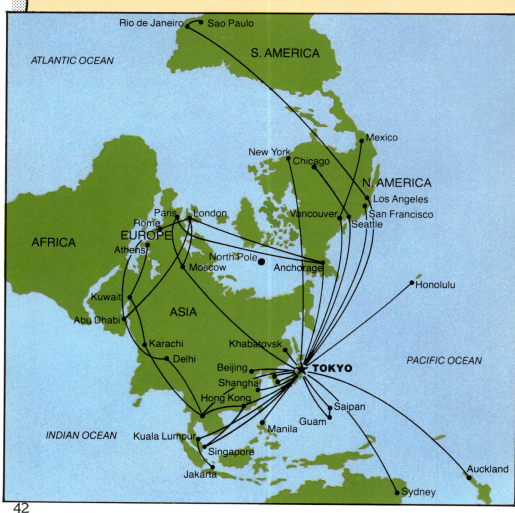

This view of the world may appear unusual to us but it is the one usually chosen for showing air routes. It shows some of the Japan Air Lines routes that link Japan with other countries.

Which do you think is quickest to get to: the US or Europe? What ways or routes of travelling to Europe or the US existed before aeroplanes were invented?

Communications studies. The Japanese are always happy to spend money on the most modern equipment.

Worker and machine work together on the production line for Toyota, third biggest car manufacturer in the world. ▼

Books to Read

There are a great many books about Japan. But a lot of them are about Japanese art and traditions. They don't tell you much about how modern Japanese people live and work. However, the following four do. The first three are written for children.

A Family in Japan,
P.O. Jacobsen and P.S. Kristensen, Wayland, 1984.
Japan: the land and its people, Richard Tames, Macdonald Educational, 1986 (new edition).
We live in Japan,
Kazuhide Kawamata, Wayland, 1984.

You might also enjoy **Japan**, in the Time-Life Library of Nations series (1985), although it is written for adults. It has some excellent pictures, showing life in modern Japan.

Things to do

Have an abacus race In Japan, a real expert on an abacus, or soroban, can add huge columns of figures in a few seconds – even faster than on a calculator. How fast can you go on an abacus? Have you ever tried timing yourself? Practise using the abacus and if you feel confident, have a race with a friend.

Count cars When you are next in a car park with a friend, write down how many cars you can count in five minutes. How many Japanese ones can your friend count?

Go visiting If you live in London, visit the Japan Information Centre, 9 Grosvenor Square, W1. Collect their 'Japan' poster and 'Japan Today' booklet, and copies of **Japan Pictorial** magazine.

Time chart

The beginnings of Japanese big business go back over a hundred years and more. Here are some important dates along the way.

1853 The ships of US Commodore Matthew Perry arrive off Japan.

1858 Japan opens five ports to foreign ships and signs trade agreements with western countries.

1866 Revolution destroys the power of Japan's military rulers or shoguns.

1868 Emperor Meiji takes power and starts plans to modernise the country.

1914–1918 Japan fights on the side of Britain and France in World War One.

1939 World War Two begins.

1941 Japan, fighting on the side of the Germans, destroys the US fleet at Pearl Harbor, in Hawaii.

1945 US drops atomic bombs on Hiroshima and Nagasaki. Japan surrenders and is occupied for seven years by the Allies.

1950 War breaks out in Korea. Japan is asked to supply US and United Nations forces with equipment, transport, and housing. This helps Japanese industry to start up again.

Mid-1950s to 1973 The 'economic miracle' happens: Japan's wealth goes up by at least a tenth every year. This is much faster than that of other countries.

1973–1974 International oil prices shoot up. Japan, which relies heavily on imported oil, has to pay three times as much for it. The growth in the country's wealth stops. It later starts again, but the 'miracle' has finished.

Keywords

Hiroko-chan Hiroko, dear. 'Chan', added on to a name, expresses affection.

Juku Private school that gives children extra tuition before their exams.

Karuta Card game that is played rather like Snap, but matched cards are discarded, not collected. The winner is the player who gets rid of all his or her cards first.

Kimono Traditional Japanese robe, still worn at home and for special occasions.

Mochi Rice cakes; part of the traditional New Year meal.

Moshi, moshi 'Hallo, who's speaking?' (on the 'phone).

Okasan Mother, mum. Japanese children also say 'Mama'.

Omedeto Well done, or congratulations.

Pagoda Temple building with several storeys. The roof of each storey sticks out some way from the main building.

Paternalism Like a father looking after his children. Big Japanese companies are famous for their paternalism to their workers: they train and then employ them for life, often giving them cheap housing and other benefits.

Roma-ji The Roman alphabet, called after Rome, as used in western Europe.

Shoguns Military rulers of Japan for over 600 years before the Meiji Restoration. There were several shogun families, of which the Tokugawas were the last and the most famous. It was a Tokugawa shogun who, in 1639, would not let most foreigners into the country.

Soroban Japanese abacus in use in Japan for over 500 years.

Tanaka-san Mr Tanaka. Added to a name, 'san' is a word that shows respect. It can also mean 'Mrs' or 'Miss'.

Yen The unit of Japanese currency. There were about 300 to the pound in 1986.

Index

Illustrations appear in **bold** type

Abacus 21, **21**, 43, 44
Air routes **42**
Alaska 38
Allies 44
America (USA) 30, 34, **35**, 40, **42**, 44
Army 20
Atomic bombs 44

Britain 15, 26, 32, 34, **37**, 40, 44
Business **8**, **9**, 14, 26, **31**, 32, 40, 44

Calculators 8, 14, 21, 43
Cameras 8, 14, 37
Commuter train **13**
Company 10, **11**, 12, **13**, 14, 24, 26, **27**, 34, 44
Computers 8, 12, **43**

Diet (Parliament) 37
Discount shops 8, **9**

Education 14, 15, 20, 30, 32, 33
Electronics **9**, 12
Emperor 17, 20
England 34, 36, 38, **39**
English language 28, 29
Europe 17, 28, **42**, 44
Exams 28, 29, **29**, 30, 32, 34, 36, 44
Export **37**, **39**, **41**

Factories 8, **9**, 12, 14, **17**, 20, **25**, 34
Farming 26
Fashion **37**
Flats 10, **11**, 24

Golf 10, 41

Hiroshima **19**, 44
Hitachi 15
Homework (*juku*) **29**
Honda **13**
Houses 10, **11**, 44

Industry **14**, 20, 32, **35**, 40, 44

Japan Air Lines **11**
Japanese Revolution 20
Jumbotron TV **15**

Karuta (card game) 24, 28, 44
Kimono 16, 17, 22, 44
Kobe 18, **19**
Korea 40, 44
Kyoto 18, 19, **19**

London 38, 39, **42**

Machinery **17**
Medical care 15
Meiji, Emperor **17**, **18**, 20, **21**, **25**, 26, **37**, 44
Meiji Restoration 17, 40, 44
Mines 20
Modernisation **17**, **27**, 44
Mori, Hanae **25**
Motorcycles **41**
Mutsuhito **21**

Nagasaki **19**, **21**, 44
Nagoya 18, 19, **19**
Nakasone, Yasuhiro 40
Narita Airport 38
New Year 16, 18, 22, 44

Osaka 18, 19, **19**, 28, 34, 38

Pagoda 10, 44
Paternalism 15, 44
Pearl Harbour 44

Perry, Matthew (Sea Commodore) **35**, 44
Portuguese 40
Pottery 25

Railway 10, **13**, **18**, 20
Revolution 44
Rice 27
Robots **17**

School 28, 29, **29**, 30, **31**, 32, 33, **33**, 34, 44
Shinkansen Super Express 18
Shipyards 20
Shoguns 20, **21**, 44
Silk 16, **16**, 17, **23**
Skiing 10, **11**
Soldiers **35**
Sony **15**, **35**
Spinning mills 20
Supertanker 15, **15**

Technology **15**, **17**, 21
Tokyo 8, 19, **19**, **21**, 30, **31**, **35**, **37**, **38**, **42**
Toyota **39**, **43**
Trade **19**, 20, **21**, **35**, 44
Traditions 22
Transport **19**, **37**, 44
TV 12, 14, 34, **41**
Typhoon 10

United Nations 44
University 29, **29**, 32, 33, **33**

Walkman **35**
Women 24, **25**, 27
World War One 44
World War Two 14, **14**, 20, **35**, **37**, 40, 44

Yen 9, **13**, 44
Yokohama 19, **19**, **37**

Illustrations
Julia Osorno 13, 27, 33
Gary Rees 4–5, 8–9, 10–11, 12–13, 16–17, 18–19, 22–23, 24–25, 28–29, 30–31, 34–35, 36–37, 38–39
Raymond Turvey, maps 4, 19, 41

Photographs
Barnaby's Picture Library: 19
Stuart Bonney Agency: 39R
British Library: 35T
Coca Cola Co, Courtesy of the: 40
Hideo Fujimori: 41R
Sally & Richard Greenhill: 35B
Robert Harding Picture Library: Cover (inset), 17B
Hutchison Picture Library: N. Hadfield 11T, M. MacIntyre 15B
Japan Graphic Inc.: 21B
Japan Information Centre: 23B, 29
Japanese National Tourist Office: 9, 11B
Keystone-Mast Collection, California Museum of Photography: 25TR, 27
Kenichi Komatsu: 28–9
Mansell Collection: 18–19, 21T, 26–7
National Archives, USA: 14–15
Orion: 9B, 42–3
Photo Source: 15T
Popperfoto: Cover, 8, 16–17, 17T, 23T, 25TL, 35M, 36–37, 37T
Power Pix: 33
Rex Features: 12–13, 31B, 31M, 37B, 41L
Eisuke Shimauchi: 32
Frank Spooner Pictures: 25B
Tokyo Shoseki Co. Ltd: 31T
Topham Picture Library: 13
Toyota: 39L, 43
Victoria & Albert Museum, Courtesy of the Board of Trustees: 20–21
Zefa: 11M

The author and publishers would like to thank the staff of the Japan Information Centre, London, for their invaluable assistance with this book. Other important sources of information include: G. C. Allen's *A short economic history of modern Japan* (Allen & Unwin), *Japan (The Economist)*, *Japan 1984* (Keizai Koho Center, Tokyo), *Japan Pictorial*, *The Sunday Times*, *The Times*, and the publications of the Foreign Press Center, Tokyo, especially *The Japanese family*.

BORDERS REGIONAL